A Pudding Book

If you keep this little book
In your kitchen for your cook,
No longer need you sighing say:
"What pudding shall we have to-day?"

from *The Everyday Pudding Book*

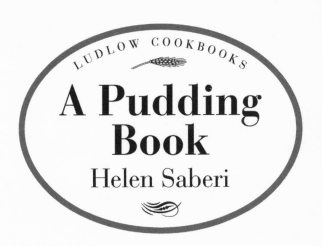

LUDLOW COOKBOOKS

A Pudding Book

Helen Saberi

EXCELLENT PRESS
in association with
LUDLOW BOOKBINDERS

Excellent Press
9 Lower Raven Lane
Ludlow SY 8 1 BW

©2006, Helen Saberi and Excellent Press

Printed in the UK by Woolnough
Bookbinding Ltd, 2006

ISBN 1 900318 30 X

Introduction to Puddings

This little book aims to give a small selection of varied, interesting or favourite sweet puddings from an historical or modern point of view. Many are interesting because they have been named after a person, including royalty or after a place perhaps where the pudding was first invented or evolved.

Great Britain is renowned for its puddings in all their glory and variation. Each county has its own specialities. To define the term pudding is very difficult for it can mean many things.

The dictionary gives the following definition:

> A cooked dish consisting of various sweet and savoury ingredients, esp. as enclosed within a flour-based crust or mixed with flour, eggs, etc., and boiled or steamed; a baked batter mixture. Now also, the sweet course of a meal.

This definition eliminates a number of other dishes which are types of pudding, such as milk puddings, fruit puddings and so on.

Boiled puddings:
When the pudding cloth was introduced around the beginning of the 17th century this opened the way for a number of puddings to be invented. One such was a sweet suet pudding called Cambridge pudding (or College pudding).

Steamed puddings:
With the advent of the 20th century and changes in lifestyle including the more widespread use of the modern oven, old-fashioned 'boiled' puddings and the use of the 'pudding-cloth' were replaced by easier methods of steaming or baking.

Baked puddings:
Baked puddings have also been around for a long time but in modern times, I think, are more popular than steamed as they are easier and quicker to make. Many steamed pudding recipes have been converted to the easier baked method. Baked puddings include the important category of many bread puddings, see below.

Bread puddings:
Bread puddings include bread whether in the form of breadcrumbs or pieces or slices of bread. Sometimes the bread is buttered and then becomes known as a bread and butter pudding. Sometimes the role of the bread is simply to be a base or case for, say fruit, as in Summer Pudding. They can fall in the category of baked or milk puddings but some are fried and can be served cold.

Milk puddings:
These can be flour or bread-based or in the form of rice, macaroni, sago and tapioca. They can be baked, or simmered on top of the stove. They can be served hot or cold.

Fruit puddings:
These include many baked dishes which are served hot although there are many exceptions as some puddings can be served cold such as Summer Pudding.

Batter puddings:
These are puddings made with a batter mix, often incorporating fruit.

Note: All recipes serve 4 unless otherwise stated.

BOILED AND STEAMED PUDDINGS

T he two methods of boiling and steaming puddings are illustrated below. For boiled puddings (top picture) the dough or mixture is wrapped in a floured pudding cloth. It is then tied with string and lowered into a pan of boiling water. It is then gently boiled, usually for several hours. A good tip is to tie the string to a handle of the pot as this makes it easier to retrieve the pudding.

A steamed pudding is cooked in a basin which is covered by a cloth. The water should come three quarters of the way up the sides of the basin.

Other tips for steaming:
- Put on the steamer with the base half-filled with water so that this is boiling by the time the pudding is made. If you do not have a steamer, fill a large saucepan with water to come halfway up the pudding basin. Bring this to the boil.
- Always grease the pudding basin well, and put a round of greased greaseproof paper in the base.
- Cut double greaseproof paper or a piece of foil to cover the pudding basin and grease well. Put pleats in the greaseproof paper or foil to allow the pudding to rise.
- Fill the basin not more than two-thirds full with mixture.

- Keep the water in the steamer boiling steadily and have a kettle of boiling water ready to top it up regularly or as necessary. The steamer should not be allowed to boil dry.
- If you are using a saucepan, put an old saucer, a trivet or crossed skewers in the base to keep the basin off the bottom. Keep the water gently bubbling so that the basin just wobbles.
- There are dozens of variations on the basic steamed pudding, and by adding different ingredients to the mixture or using different flavourings or toppings you can ring the changes almost indefinitely.

****

ROLY-POLY PUDDINGS

Roly-Poly puddings are perhaps the best known of all steamed puddings and long time favourite of many a schoolboy. There are variations on the theme such as: jam (the traditional ones are raspberry, strawberry or apricot), syrup, treacle, lemon, ginger and mincemeat. A Roly-Poly is also known as Bolster Pudding and 'a dog in a blanket'. The Roly-Poly can be boiled, steamed or baked. The recipe below is for Jam Roly Poly.

175 g self-raising flour
1/2 level teaspoon salt
75 g shredded suet
about 7 tablespoons cold water
4–6 tablespoons jam
a little milk

Half fill a steamer with water and put it on to boil.

Make the pastry by mixing together the flour, salt and suet. Add enough cold water to give a light, elastic dough and knead very lightly until smooth.

Grease a piece of foil 23 by 33 cm. Roll out the pastry into an oblong about 23 by 25 cm. Spread the jam over the pastry, leaving 0.5 cm clear along each edge. Brush the edges with milk and roll the pastry up evenly, starting from the short end. Place the roll on the greased foil and wrap the foil round the roll loosely, to allow room for the pudding to expand. Seal the edges well. Steam in the steamer over rapidly boiling water for 1 1/2 to 2 hours.

Remove from the foil and serve sliced with custard.

To bake this pudding, if preferred, place in the oven uncovered at 200°C, 400°F, gas mark 6 for about 40 minutes.

VARIATIONS:

Mincemeat. Add the finely grated rind of 1 orange to the dough and spread the pastry with mincemeat instead of jam and continue as in the recipe above.

Lemon. Add the finely grated rind of a lemon to the pastry. Roll out and spread with 4–6 tablespoons lemon curd.

Ginger. Put a good layer of brown sugar over the pastry (except the edges), dust with ground ginger and sprinkle liberally with lemon juice with some of the lemon rind grated in.

Syrup. Mix 4 tablespoons golden syrup with 3 tablespoons fresh white breadcrumbs and spread over the pastry as above.

Treacle. Mix 4 tablespoons treacle with 4 tablespoons sugar, the juice and grated zest of 1/2 lemon and some dried or grated fresh ginger spread over the pastry as above.

SPOTTED DICK

This is a popular suet pudding which is 'spotted' with currants or raisins. There are variations on this pudding which can also be of the roly-poly type (see page 8) and can be boiled, baked or, as in this recipe, steamed.

100 g self-raising flour	50 g currants
pinch salt	50 g mixed peel
50 g Atora suet	1 egg, beaten
50 g sugar	4 tablespoon milk

Mix together the dry ingredients. Add the egg and sufficient milk to produce a smooth dropping consistency. Transfer the mixture to a greased 500 ml pudding basin. Cover with pleated greaseproof paper and/or foil and steam for 1 1/2 to 2 hours.

Turn out and serve hot with custard.

****

DROWNED (BOILED) BABY

The following recipe comes from *Lobscouse* and *Spotted Dog*, which gives recipes from the galley of Captain Jack Aubrey, an 18th century seaman whose adventures are marvellously described in Patrick O'Brian's novels.

The gunroom's feast for the Captain was if anything more copious than that of the day before: ... the gunroom cook, by means known to himself alone, had conserved the makings of a superb suet pudding of the kind called boiled baby in the service, known to be Jack Aubrey's favourite form of food, and it came in on a scrubbed scuttle-cover to the sound of cheering.

- The Nutmeg of Consolation, 227

Jack reached the galley, inspected the coppers, the harness-casks, the slush-tubs, the three hundredweight of plum-duff preparing for Sunday dinner; and with some satisfaction he noticed his own private drowned baby simmering in its long kettle. But this satisfaction was as private as his pudding.

- The Ionian Mission, 136

Serves 12-16

4 cups flour
1/4 cup sugar
1/2 teaspoon salt
1 teaspoon ground cinnamon

11/2 cups raisins
1/2 pound suet, finely grated
ice water

In a large bowl, mix the flour, sugar, salt, and cinnamon. Stir in the raisins, (the flour will coat them and keep them from clumping together). Mix in the suet.

Work in 1-2 tablespoons ice water. Continue gradually adding ice water until you have a stiff paste (it will probably take about a cup of water, but this will vary depending on temperature, humidity, the dryness of your flour, etc.). Work it with your hands until it forms a ball. Turn it out onto a well-floured board. Cover with a damp cloth and let rest for 5 minutes.

Knead the dough until it is shiny and elastic (6-8 minutes), cover again, let rest another 5 minutes, then knead again for 1-2 minutes.

Shape the dough into a nice, fat, vaguely cylindrical lump. Wrap the pudding fairly loosely in a well-floured cloth. Tie securely at both ends (we usually also tie a string loosely around the middle, to keep the cloth from gaping). Immerse the pudding in a pot of rapidly boiling water and cook for 21/2 hours, replenishing the water as necessary.

To serve, untie and unroll the cloth. Turn the pudding out onto a board or platter. Serve hot, accompanied by Custard Sauce.

11

FIG PUDDING

This recipe comes from Col. Kenney-Herbert's *Culinary Jottings for Madras* (1885).

Take a quarter of a pound of finely grated breadcrumbs, half a pound of minced dried figs, three ounces of sugar, six ounces of chopped suet, and a little grated nutmeg. Mix a teaspoonful of baking powder with an ounce of flour, add this to the other ingredients with four eggs well beaten, moisten with a little milk sufficiently to form a firm paste, turn the mixture into a buttered mould, and boil for three hours.

LIME SAUCE to accompany the above. – Put three table-spoonfuls of sugar into a sauce-pan with a breakfast-cupful of water, and the very finely peeled rind of a lime, simmer for twenty minutes, then add the juice of two limes and a liqueur glass of any liqueur, brandy, or rum, strain and serve. A drop or two of cochineal will improve the colour of the sauce.

GINGER PUDDING

200 g self raising flour
pinch of salt
2 teaspoons ground ginger
50 g margarine
50 g sugar
25 g stem ginger, chopped roughly
2 tablespoons treacle
2 eggs

Mix together the flour, salt. Ginger and stem ginger. Rub in the margarine and mix in the other ingredients.

Place the mixture in a greased 750 ml pudding basin.

Cover with greaseproof paper or foil and steam for 2 hrs.

Turn out and serve hot with custard.

SNOWDON PUDDING

Eliza Acton (1845) gives a recipe for this pudding telling us this is a 'Genuine Receipt' and that 'This pudding is constantly served to travellers at the hotel at the foot of the mountain from which it derives its name.'

Ornament a well buttered mould or basin with some fine raisins split open and stoned, but not divided, pressing the cut side on the butter to make them adhere; next, mix half a pound of very finely minced beef-kidney suet, with half a pound of breadcrumbs, and an ounce and a half of rice-flour, a pinch of salt, and six ounces of lemon marmalade, or of orange when the lemon cannot be procured; and six ounces of pale brown sugar, six thoroughly whisked eggs, and the grated rinds of two lemons. Beat the whole until all the ingredients are perfectly mixed, pour it gently into the mould, cover it with a buttered paper and a floured cloth, and boil it for one hour and a half. It will turn out remarkably well if carefully prepared. Half the quantity given above will fill a mould or basin which will contain rather more than a pint, and will be sufficiently boiled in ten minutes less than an hour. To many tastes a slight diminution in the proportion of suet would be an improvement to the pudding; and the substitution of pounded sugar for the brown, might likewise be considered so. Both the suet and eggs used for it, should be as fresh as possible.

Wine sauce, arrowroot, German sauce, or any other of the sweet pudding sauces ... may be poured over, or sent to table with it. (See next page).

Wine Sauce for Sweet Puddings

Boil gently together for ten or fifteen minutes the very thin rind of half a small lemon, about an ounce and a half of sugar, and a wineglassful of water. Take out the lemon- peel, and stir into the sauce until it has boiled for one minute, an ounce of butter smoothly mixed with a large half-teaspoonful of flour; add a wineglassful and a half of sherry or Madeira, or other good white wine, and when quite hot serve the sauce without delay.

****

Some recipes advocate a rich white sauce for Snowdon Pudding which when poured over the pudding resembles the snow on the mountain. Here is my own recipe. A little brandy, rum or other flavouring could be added at the final stage.

1 heaped tablespoon cornflour
300 ml milk
25 g caster sugar
25 g butter

Blend the cornflour in a small basin with a little of the milk. Place the remaining milk in a saucepan with the butter and stir in the cornflour mixture. Slowly bring to the boil, stirring constantly and boil gently until thickened. Add the sugar and simmer gently for about 3 minutes. Serve hot, poured over the pudding.

Sussex Pond Pudding

When this steamed pudding is turned out and cut open a lovely buttery/lemony mixture flows out and makes a 'pond'.

350 g self raising flour
1/2 level teaspoon salt
175 g shredded suet
100 g butter
100 g Demerara sugar
1 large, thin skinned lemon

Mix together the flour, salt and suet. Add enough cold water to make a light, elastic dough (about 175 ml). Knead lightly until smooth. Set aside a quarter of the dough to make the lid.

With the rest of the dough, roll it out on a floured surface to a circle which should be 2.5 cm larger all round than the diameter of a 1.5 litre pudding basin. Line the basin with this pastry. Into the centre of the hollow place half the butter which should first be cut up in pieces along with half of the sugar.

Prick the lemon all over with a skewer and place on top of the butter and sugar. Cover with the remaining sugar and butter.

Roll out the reserved quarter of the suet pastry to a circle to fit the top of the pudding. Seal the edges by dampening. Cover with greaseproof paper and foil.

Steam for about 4 hours. Remove the wrapping and turn out on to a warm serving dish.

CABINET PUDDING

There are numerous variations for Cabinet Pudding, hot or cold. According to Alan Davidson in *The Oxford Companion to Food* (1999) the political link, though unexplained, is constant. Another name for this pudding is Diplomat Pudding.

The recipe below is taken from *Everyday Desserts* by Olive Green (1911), who wrote a series of practical cookery books in the early 20th century.

Fill a mould nearly full with alternate layers of stale sponge cake, macaroons, and preserved or candied fruit cut into bits. Fill with an uncooked custard made with the yolks of three eggs, two whole eggs, half a cupful of sugar, two cupfuls of milk, two tablespoons of Madeira, and the grated rind of half a lemon. Set the mould in a pan of hot water to reach to three-fourths its height. Simmer for two hours, turn out, and serve with Lemon Sauce.

Olive gives no less than 13 lemon sauces plus 1 lemon butter sauce and 2 lemon cream sauces. A difficult choice but going on the principle I admire, the simplest is the best – here is Lemon Sauce - I.

Cook to the consistency of syrup one cupful of sugar, one tablespoonful of butter, and half a cupful of water. Take from the fire, add a tablespoonful of lemon-juice, and a little of the grated peel.

PARADISE PUDDING

There are a number of recipes going by this name. This one is adapted from *The Everyday Pudding Book*.

3 apples	*a little grated nutmeg*
2 eggs	*rind of 1 lemon and some of*
75 g breadcrumbs	*the juice*
75 g sugar	*pinch of salt*
75 g currants	*1 wineglass brandy*

Pare and core and cut up the apples. Sprinkle the apples with the lemon juice in a bowl and then with the 'dry' ingredients. Beat the eggs and mix them in. Lastly stir in the brandy. Butter a basin and pour the mixture in. Cover with a buttered paper to keep out the moisture and tie down with a cloth. Allow for swelling. Boil for two hours.

Serve plain or with a brandy sauce as below:

25 g butter
50 g sugar
rind of 1 lemon
25 g cornflour
300 ml milk
1 wineglass brandy

Melt the butter in a saucepan. Sift the flour in slowly, stirring all the time. Now add the milk, sugar, and the grated rind of lemon. Stir for about five minutes, allowing it to boil gently. Take it off the fire and add the brandy. Strain through a sieve and pour a little over the top of the pudding to garnish and the rest into a sauceboat.

BAKED PUDDINGS

BAKEWELL PUDDING

The following comes from the witty pen of E S Dallas, in *Kettner's Book of the Table* (1877).

BAKEWELL PUDDING is the glory of Derbyshire. One might have expected some miracle of excellence for the palate from the ducal residence of Chatsworth, with all its fame and its splendour, and the highest fountain jet in the world. But, although a Duchess of Devonshire once kissed a butcher, the great house of Cavendish has done nothing for our tables which can compare with the humble achievement of some unknown genius in the small town of Bakewell, nigh to the prodigious Chatsworth.

Line a pie-dish with a light paste*. Place on this a thickish layer of any preserved fruit from the most common to the most refined – let us say peaches or apricots. The Bakewellians are in the habit of intermingling this with candied citron or orange-peel, cut into thin strips – a part of the ceremony which may be safely omitted. Make a custard of six yolks and three whites of eggs, from four to five ounces of clarified butter, six ounces of sifted sugar, and three spoonfuls of what the Bakewellians call lemon-brandy – that is, brandy which has been flavoured by long maceration with the zest of lemons. A little of the zest of lemon may be used instead, or any other flavour that may be preferred. Pour the custard over and among the apricot jam, and bake the pudding in a moderate oven for three-quarters of an hour.

*Use ready made thin puff pastry

Plum Meringue Pudding

This recipe is also good made with cherries.

450 g cooking plums, stoned and halved
juice and rind of 1 orange
75 g brown sugar
142 ml water
75–150 g breadcrumbs or bread cubes
2 egg yolks
1 level teaspoon cinnamon
2 egg whites
110 g caster sugar

Place the plums or cherries in a pan and add the orange juice and rind and the sugar. Simmer gently for a few minutes.

Place the bread into an ovenproof dish, then pour the hot syrup from the fruit over it. Leave to soak for about 10 minutes. Stir in the egg yolks. Then add the drained fruit and sprinkle with the cinnamon.

Bake in the centre of the oven 375°F, 190°C, gas mark 4 for about 30 minutes or until set. Remove from the oven and turn the heat down to 300°F, 150°C, gas mark 2.

Meanwhile make the meringue topping. Whip up the egg whites in a bowl until very stiff. Gradually beat in half of the sugar, then fold in the rest.

Pile the meringue on to the top of the bread and fruit.

Return to the cool oven and bake for a further 30 minutes until the meringue is a pale golden brown.

Can be served hot or cold with fresh cream.

RHUBARB CRUMBLE

C rumbles can be made from all kinds of fruit, so instead of rhubarb, you could use apples, plums, gooseberries, blackcurrants or apricots according to the season or choice.

900 g rhubarb
cinnamon or ginger
175 g sugar
75 g butter
175 g plain flour
a little grated orange rind (optional)

Wash the rhubarb stalks, top and tail them and remove and discard any tough strings. Cut into 2 cm lengths. Place in a deep ovenproof dish and sprinkle over 75 g of the sugar and about a teaspoon of powdered cinnamon or ginger. Add two tablespoons of cold water.

Rub the butter into the flour until the mixture is the texture of fine crumbs and stir in the rest of the sugar. Mix in the grated orange rind, if used.

Sprinkle the crumble mixture on top of the rhubarb and bake in the oven at 190°C, 375°F, gas mark 6 for about 30 or 40 minutes or until crisp and golden brown on top. Serve with custard or cream.

Eve's Pudding

450 g cooking apples,
peeled and cored
75 g Demerara sugar
grated rind of 1 lemon
1 tablespoon water

75 g butter
75 g caster sugar
1 egg, beaten
125 g self raising flour
milk to mix

Slice the apples thinly into a greased 900 ml ovenproof dish and sprinkle the Demerara sugar and grated lemon rind over them. Add the water. Cream the fat and sugar until pale and fluffy. Add the egg a little at a time, beating well after each addition. Fold in the flour with a little milk to give a dropping consistency and spread the mixture over the apples. Bake in the oven at 180°C, 350°F, gas mark 4 for about 40 to 45 minutes, until the apples are tender and the sponge mixture cooked.

Serve with custard.

****

Gooseberry Pudding

This recipe comes from the *Experienced English Housekeeper* by Elizabeth Raffald (1769). Many authorities consider Mrs Raffald's book from Manchester to be the finest cook book of the 18th century.

Scald half a pint of green gooseberries in water till they are soft, put them into a sieve to drain. When cold work them through a hair sieve with the back of a clean wooden spoon, add to them half a pound of sugar and the same of butter, four ounces of Naples [boudoir] biscuits. Beat six eggs very well, and then mix all together and beat them a quarter of an hour, pour it in an earthen dish without paste. Half an hour will bake it.

PINEAPPLE UPSIDE-DOWN PUDDING

This is a well known favourite.

50 g butter
50 g brown sugar
226 g can pineapple rings, drained
100 g butter
100 g caster sugar
2 eggs, beaten
175 g self raising flour
30-45 ml pineapple juice

Grease an 18 cm round cake tin. Cream together the butter and brown sugar and spread it over the bottom of the tin. Arrange the rings of pineapple on top of this layer. Cream together the remaining fat and sugar until pale and fluffy. Add the beaten egg a little at a time and beat well after each addition. Fold in the flour, adding some pineapple juice to give a dropping consistency, and spread on top of the pineapple rings. Bake in the oven at 180°F, 350°F, gas mark 4 for about 45 minutes. Turn out on to a dish and serve with a pineapple sauce made by thickening the remaining juice with a little cornflour. Or serve with whipped cream or custard.

Rhubarb and Ginger Cobbler

A cobbler is a sort of fruit pie made with a thick scone-like crust. It can be made with all kinds of fruit such as cherries, plums, apples, blackberries etc. This one is made with rhubarb and the 'cobbler' is flavoured with ginger which makes a nice change. The dish originated in the USA.

450 g rhubarb
2 tablespoons soft brown sugar
2 tablespoons water
175 g self raising flour
1 teaspoon ground ginger
pinch salt
50 g butter
25 g caster sugar
1 egg, beaten
milk

Place the rhubarb, cut into short lengths, in a pan and add the brown sugar and water. Simmer slowly to soften the fruit. Transfer to a casserole dish and leave to cool.

Mix the self raising flour with the ginger and salt. Rub in the butter until it resembles fine breadcrumbs. Now add the beaten egg and enough milk to make a soft dough.

Turn out on to a floured board and roll out to a thickness of 1 cm. Cut into rounds with a cutter of 5 cm diameter. The dough should make about 12 scones.

Arrange the scones on top of the fruit, overlapping slightly. Brush with a little milk to glaze.

Place in a preheated oven at 190°C, 360°F, gas mark 5 for about 30 minutes.

APRICOT PUDDING

This recipe comes from *Adam's Luxury and Eve's Cookery* of 1744 and appears as below but it is followed by a modern version which is easier to follow.

Coddle six large Apricots very tender, break them small, and sweeten them to your Taste. When they are cold, add six Eggs, but only two Whites, a little Cream; put it in Puff-Paste, and bake it. You may thus make any Fruit Pudding.

****

6 large apricots
sugar to taste
4 egg yolks
2 egg whites
a little cream
puff pastry

Steam the apricots in a little water until soft. Chop them up into small pieces and sweeten to taste. Leave to cool, then beat in the eggs and cream.

Line a pie dish or plate with puff pastry.

Put the mixture in the pastry and bake in the oven at 190°C, 375°F, gas mark 5 for about half an hour until the pastry is cooked and the pudding firm.

Chocolate Pudding with Prunes and Brandy
With a Crème Fraiche and Brandy Sauce

M y friend Hilary Hyman gave me this recipe and it is very good. It is a soufflé which is allowed to sink into a rich, dark, squidgy pudding.

Serves 6-8

For the prunes:
350 g pitted ready-to-eat prunes
275 ml water
150 ml brandy

For the soufflé:
225 g good dark dessert chocolate
110 g unsalted butter
1 tablespoon brandy
4 eggs separated
110 caster sugar
icing sugar

Soak the prunes overnight. Place them in a saucepan with the water, bring them to a simmer and then let them simmer gently for about 30 minutes. Pour the prunes and their cooking liquid into a bowl and stir in the brandy while still warm. Leave to cool, then cover the bowl and leave to chill in the refrigerator overnight.

Grease a 20 cm spring-form cake tin and line with silicone paper. Preheat the oven to 170°C, 325°F, gas mark 3.

Now make the soufflé. Break the chocolate into squares and place them with the butter in a bowl fitted over a saucepan containing some barely simmering water, making sure the bottom of the bowl does not touch the water. The chocolate will slowly melt and then stir until the mixture becomes smooth and glossy. Now remove the bowl from the heat and add the brandy. Leave to cool.

Next take a large bowl and combine the egg yolks and caster sugar in it. Whisk together with an electric hand whisk until the mixture will drop off the whisk making ribbon-like trails when you lift it up – about 5 minutes.

Now remove 18 of the soaked prunes and cut each one in half. Combine these with the whisked egg mixture along with the melted chocolate.

Whisk up the egg whites with a clean whisk until they form soft peaks. Fold these carefully into the chocolate mixture. Spoon this mixture into the prepared tin and bake in the centre of the oven for about 30 minutes or until the centre feels springy to the touch.

Remove from the oven and allow the soufflé to cool in the tin. It will fall very slowly. When quite cold, remove from the tin, peel off the paper, then cover and chill for several hours.

Dust with icing sugar. Cut in small slices and serve with the sauce.

For the sauce:
The remainder of the soaked prunes
150 ml crème fraiche

Liquidise the reserved prunes with their liquid. Place the puree in a bowl and stir in the crème fraiche creating a sort of marbling effect.

Chocolate Pudding

This chocolate pudding is much simpler than the previous one, but nevertheless still good.

50 g self-raising flour
50 g caster sugar
25 g cocoa powder
1/2 teaspoon cinnamon

1/2 teaspoon baking powder
50 g soft margarine
2 eggs
a little vanilla essence

For the sauce:
75 g soft dark brown sugar
15 g cocoa powder
125 ml warm water

To serve:
Icing sugar
25 g toasted hazelnuts, chopped

Grease an 1 litre ovenproof glass dish or pudding basin. Preheat the oven to 180°C, 350°F, gas mark 4.

Mix the flour, sugar, cocoa, cinnamon and baking powder in a bowl. In another bowl beat together the eggs, margarine and essence. Now sift the flour and other dry ingredients on to the egg mixture and mix in. Beat well.

Place in the ovenproof dish.

Now make the sauce. Blend the sugar and cocoa with the water and carefully pour over the pudding mixture.

Bake in the preheated oven for about 30 minutes. The pudding, when cooked, will have risen well and the sauce will be at the bottom of the bowl.

Remove from the oven, dust with the icing sugar and sprinkle with the toasted hazelnuts.

STICKY TOFFEE PUDDING

T his pudding is said to have been devised in the Lake District in the 1960s. However, it is also said that the original concept for the recipe came from a farm wife in Lancashire. Scotland too has staked a claim saying that it originated in the Udny Arms Hotel in Newburgh. Whatever its origin this rich pudding has become popular in pubs and restaurants all over Britain.

Serves 6-8

110 g chopped dates
75 g butter
150 g caster sugar
175 g flour
2 eggs

175 ml boiling water
1 teaspoon strong coffee
1 teaspoon bicarbonate
of soda

Toffee sauce:
175 g brown sugar
75 g butter
110 ml double cream

Grease and line a baking dish about 10 by 15 cm. Preheat the oven to 180°C, 350°F, gas mark 4.

Place the dates, butter, sugar and flour in a bowl and mix together to resemble breadcrumbs. In a bowl mix the boiling water, the coffee and the bicarbonate of soda. Add this to the dry ingredients. Now beat in the eggs, one at a time, mixing well to incorporate air. The mixture should have a batter consistency. Pour the mixture into the baking dish and bake in the preheated oven for about 30 to 35 minutes until firm to the touch.

For the sauce, melt the butter and sugar over a low heat until dissolved. Slowly add the cream and bring to the boil.

Serve over the pudding, or if preferred, separately.

BREAD PUDDINGS

A BREAD AND BUTTER PUDDING

An early recipe for bread and butter pudding is in Hannah Glasse's *The Art of Cookery made Plain and Easy* (1747) I like her idea of adding rose-water.

Take a Penny Loaf, and cut it into thin Slices of bread and Butter, as you do for Tea. Butter your Dish as you cut them, lay Slices all over the Dish, then strew a few Currans, clean washed and picked, then a Row of Bread and Butter, then a few Currans, and so on, till all your Bread and Butter is in; then take a Pint of Milk, beat up four Eggs, a little Salt, half a Nutmeg grated, mix all together with Sugar to your Taste. Pour this over the bread, and bake it half an Hour. A Puff-paste under does best.

You may put in two Spoonfuls of Rose-water.

NEWMARKET PUDDING

In the *Cook and Housewife's Manual* (1829) Meg Dods, gives a bread and butter pudding from the headquarters of horse-racing. (It can also be called Nursery Pudding.)

Bread-and-Butter, or Newmarket Pudding.

Boil a pint and a quarter of good milk for a few minutes, with the rind of half a lemon, a stick of cinnamon, and a bay-leaf. Put in fine sugar to taste, and as the milk cools mix it gradually with the well-beat yolks of six eggs, and three of the whites separately beaten. Let this soak, and cut and butter thinly with fresh butter, slices of bread about a quarter-inch thick. Line a pudding-dish or mould neatly with the bread, and then place a layer of cleaned currants and a few raisins stoned and chopped, then again bread, and then fruit; but have the top layer of buttered bread. Pour the prepared custard through a sieve over this; let it soak for an hour, and bake or steam the pudding for a half-hour, or rather more. A few large raisins or small French plums, laid in order in the bottom of the mould, and embossed in the bread, have a good effect when the pudding is turned out.

TABITHA TICKLETOOTH'S
BREAD-AND-BUTTER PUDDING

The writer known as Tabitha Tickletooth (who was in fact the Victorian actor and dramatist Charles Selby), in *The Dinner Question* (1860), gives the following recipe for a bread and butter pudding. I like the idea of adding a little fresh or candied lemon peel and the rather clever instructions for pouring the custard in so as not to disturb the decorative effect of the currants and the peel.

Put three layers of very thin slices of bread and butter into a well buttered dish; sprinkle each layer with currants and a little fresh or candied lemon peel. (Two ounces of the former and one ounce of the latter will be sufficient for the whole pudding.)

Boil three-quarters of a pint of milk with two bay-leaves and a blade of mace ten minutes; then take out the bay leaves and mace, and having in the meantime beaten up the yolks and whites of three eggs with three-quarters of a pint of cold milk, add the hot with an ounce and a half of moist sugar.

Pour this custard gently in at one end of the dish (to prevent the currants and lemon from being disturbed); grate half a nutmeg over the top, and bake in a brisk oven three-quarters of an hour.

Hilda's Bread and Butter Pudding

This is my mother's recipe. She made it often because it was one of my father's favourite puddings.

*3-4 thin slices of
bread and butter
50 g currants or sultanas
1 tablespoon caster sugar*

*400 ml whole milk
2 eggs
ground nutmeg*

Cut the bread and butter into strips and arrange, buttered side up, in layers in a greased ovenproof dish, sprinkling the layers with the fruit and sugar. Heat the milk, but do not allow to boil. Whisk the eggs lightly and pour the milk on to them, stirring all the time. Strain the mixture over the bread, sprinkle some nutmeg on top and let the pudding stand for 15 minutes. Bake in the oven at 180°C, 350°F, gas mark 4 for 30 to 40 minutes, until set and lightly browned.

****

St. Helena Pudding

This recipe comes from *The Everyday Pudding Book* (1866). I like the fact that the bread 'sippets' are dipped in brandy before being 'strewed' with currants and lemon peel.

Cut some rather thin slices of white bread without crust; divide them into the size of small sippets; butter them on both sides, and fry them of a nice brown colour; then dip them into brandy: pack them into a buttered pie dish, strewing a few currants and lemon-peel between. Pour in a quart of new milk in which you have beaten two eggs; add some sugar; let it stand two hours to soak, then bake it for forty minutes in a moderate oven. Serve, decorated with citron-chips on the top.

OSBORNE PUDDING

A variation of bread and butter pudding. It is an interesting recipe using brown bread and marmalade.

3-4 thin slices of brown bread and butter
marmalade
1 level tablespoon caster sugar
400 ml milk
2 eggs
ground nutmeg

Spread the marmalade on to the bread and butter. Cut into strips and arrange, marmalade side up, in layers in a greased ovenproof dish. Sprinkle with the caster sugar.

Heat the milk, but do not allow to boil. Whisk the eggs lightly and pour the milk on to them, stirring all the time. Strain the mixture over the bread, sprinkle the nutmeg on the top and let the pudding stand for 15 minutes. Bake in the oven at 180°C, 350°F, gas mark 4 for 30 to 40 minutes, until set and lightly browned.

APPLE AND BLACKBERRY CHARLOTTE

A Charlotte is a pudding made in a mould lined with sponge fingers or with bread. There are two principal kinds: baked and unbaked. For winter they are usually baked and the best known is Apple Charlotte. The recipe below includes blackberries.

The name Charlotte given to this range of puddings was probably bestowed in honour of the popular Queen Charlotte who was the wife of George III in the late 18th century.

> 450 g cooking apples, peeled and cored
> 450 g blackberries
> rind and juice of 1/2 lemon
> 1/4 teaspoon cinnamon
> 50 g melted butter
> 6 slices of white bread
> 175-225 g sugar
> 2 tablespoons bread or cake crumbs

Quarter the apples. Wash and pick over the blackberries. Stew the fruit in a pan with the lemon rind, juice and cinnamon. Brush a charlotte mould or a 12.5 cm cake tin generously with melted butter. Cut the crusts off the bread. Trim one piece to a round the same size as the base of the tin, dip it into the melted butter and fit into the bottom of the tin. Dip the remaining slices of bread in the butter and arrange closely around the side of the tin, reserving one piece for the top. Add the sugar and crumbs to the stewed fruit, mix well and fill the tin. Cover with the remaining slice of bread, trimmed to fit the top of the mould. Cook in the oven at 190°C, 375°F, gas mark 5 for about an hour.

Turn out and serve with custard or cream.

Panettone Bread-and-Butter Pudding

Italy also has a tradition in bread puddings.

Half a small 500 g panettone
2-3 tablespoons candied peel
500 ml milk
250 ml double cream
4 egg yolks
2 whole eggs
125 g caster sugar

Cut the panettone into four segments, then into slices about 1 cm thick, and lay them, over-lapping, in a shallow oven-proof dish. Sprinkle with the candied peel.

Whisk together the eggs and sugar, and then the milk and cream, and pour over the panettone. Bake in a pre-heated, medium hot oven at 200°C, 400°F, gas mark 6 for about 20 minutes, by which time it should have puffed up and the custard set.

POOR KNIGHTS OF WINDSOR

Here is a rich dish or pudding of fried bread, milk, eggs, sugar and sherry, very similar to what the French call *Pain Perdu* ('Lost Bread') which dates from the Middle Ages onwards. Flavourings vary and can include nutmeg, cinnamon and rosewater. The poor Knights of Windsor were an order of military pensioners founded in 1349.

8 slices of white bread about 2.5 cm thick, crusts removed
300 ml milk
75 g caster sugar
30 ml sweet sherry
2 egg yolks
125 g butter
cinnamon or nutmeg

Cut the slices of bread into two triangles.

Pour half of the milk with 25 g of the sugar and the sherry into a shallow dish. Mix well.

Dip the bread into this mixture and soak well. Set to one side to drain on a wire rack.

Beat the egg yolks with the remaining milk and now dip the triangles of bread into this.

Heat the butter in a frying pan and fry the bread slices until golden. Place on a warmed serving dish and sprinkle with the remaining sugar which has been flavoured with cinnamon or grated nutmeg.

Serve hot or cold with whipped cream.

QUEEN OF PUDDINGS OR QUEEN'S PUDDING

T his is one of the classic English puddings which originated in the 19th century. It seems to be related to the Manchester Pudding although there are differences. A dish like the present day version apparently goes back to Sir Kenelm Digby in *The Closet of Sir Kenelm Digby Knight Opened* in 1669 in that it contained breadcrumbs combined with milk and egg yolks, part baked, and then topped with jam and meringue made from the whites and baked until done. Manchester Pudding (see next page) is different in that it has a layer of puff pastry at the bottom of the dish and does not have a meringue topping. Both variations are good.

400 ml milk
25 g butter
grated rind of 1/2 lemon
2 eggs, separated
50 g caster sugar

75 g fresh white breadcrumbs
30 ml strawberry or raspberry jam

Warm the milk, butter and lemon rind. Whisk the egg yolks and half of the sugar lightly and pour on the milk, stirring well. Strain over the breadcrumbs, pour into a greased 1.1 litre ovenproof dish and leave to stand for 15 minutes. Bake in the oven at 180°, 350°F, gas mark 4 for about 30 minutes, until lightly set. Remove from the oven. Warm the jam and spread it over the pudding. Whisk up the egg whites stiffly and add half the remaining sugar. Whisk up again and then fold in the remaining sugar. Pile this meringue on top of the jam and bake for another 15 to 20 minutes, until the meringue is lightly browned.

Manchester Pudding

T here could only be one queen who could have inspired the name and that was of course Queen Victoria, probably on one of her visits to Manchester. This recipe comes from Mrs Beeton (1861).

INGREDIENTS.- 3 oz. of grated bread, 1/2 pint of milk, a strip of lemon-peel, 4 eggs, 2 oz. of butter, sugar to taste, puff-paste, jam, 3 tablespoonfuls of brandy.

MODE.- Flavour the milk with lemon-peel, by infusing it in the milk for 1/2 hour; then strain it on to the bread crumbs, and boil it for 2 or 3 minutes; add the eggs, leaving out the whites of 2, the butter, sugar, and brandy; stir all these ingredients well together; cover a pie-dish with puff-paste, and at the bottom put a thick layer of any kind of jam; pour the above mixture, cold, on the jam, and bake the pudding for an hour. Serve cold, with a little sifted sugar sprinkled over.

****

Wet Nellie

Wet Nellie is a Liverpudlian dish. Helen Pollard in *Traditional Food East and West of the Pennines* (1991) describes it thus:

'... originally a cheap way of using stale bread and crusts. These were crumbled and mixed with suet, sugar or syrup and a little spice before baking and cutting into pieces. The bottom piece of a pile was considered the best value for money as, hopefully, the syrup would have soaked through the other layers. 'Wet' probably refers to the sticky syrup, 'Nellie' being derived from Nelson. A similar dish is known as Nelson's cake or Nelson's slice in Plymouth, and in Norfolk where Nelson was born.'

CHERRY BREAD PUDDING

This recipe has been inspired by a Turkish one.

1 kg dark red cherries, stoned
8 tablespoons Demerara sugar
juice of one lemon
12 slices of buttered bread (on both sides)
clotted cream

Place the cherries in a thick bottomed pan, add the sugar (more or less according to taste), the lemon juice. Stir well and simmer gently stirring carefully from time to time until tender.

Fry the buttered bread until golden brown on both sides. Arrange half of the bread in a pan. Pour half the cherries on top of the bread. Repeat with the remaining bread and cherries.

Cook over a low heat for about 5 minutes. Remove from the heat and allow to cool in the pan.

Remove the bread and cherries carefully from the pan with a fish slice or slotted spoon and arrange on a serving dish. Serve with clotted cream.

SUMMER PUDDING

Summer Pudding is a very traditional British dessert. One usually associates bread puddings with cold winter time. Here is one for summer.

1 kg summer fruits such as raspberries,
red currants and black currants, etc
6 slices of stale white bread, crusts removed
110-225 g sugar, according to taste and
tartness of fruits used
butter
double cream, to serve

Lightly grease a 1 litre pudding basin with the butter. Cut the bread to cover the bottom and sides of the basin and put them in place, reserving some for the top.

Place the fruits in a saucepan with a few tablespoons of water and the sugar. Cook gently until the fruit is soft. Taste, adding more sugar if necessary.

When the fruit mixture has cooled a little pour it carefully into the basin making sure not to dislodge the bread lining. The level of the fruit should be close to the top of the basin but not brimming over. Cut the remaining pieces of bread to fit on top of the fruit mixture and put them in place.

Place a plate or large saucer over the top of the basin and place a weight on to so as to compress the pudding and allow the fruit juices to soak into the bread. Leave overnight in a cool place or the fridge.

To serve, remove the weight and plate. Turn out carefully on to a serving dish and serve with thick double cream.

TIMBALE DE POIRES

A timbale is the name of a plain straight-sided mould like a charlotte mould. This recipe comes from the Namur region of Belgium.

500 g pears
200-250 g thin slices of bread (not too fresh)
125 g melted butter
100 g fine-grained brown sugar
100 ml water

Butter a charlotte mould (a plain deep mould with sloping sides). Remove the crusts from the bread and line the mould with them. Spoon a little melted butter over.

Peel, core and slice the pears thinly and spread a layer of pears over the bread. Dust with sugar and brush with a little melted butter.

Cover with another layer of bread and repeat until you have filled the mould.

Finally, pour the water over the lot, and bake in a medium oven (190°C, 375°F, gas mark 5) for about 1 hour.

Unmould and serve hot with thin fresh cream.

Apple brown Betty

This is a North American baked dessert which can be made with other fruits and then called just a brown Betty but Apple brown Betty is the favourite. It is not known who Betty was.

6 apples
a little lemon juice
2 cups brown breadcrumbs
1/2 teaspoon cinnamon
1 tablespoon sugar
75 g raisins
25 g butter
4 tablespoons golden syrup
4 tablespoons warm water

Grease an ovenproof dish with butter. Peel and core the apples and slice them, sprinkling with a little lemon juice. Add the cinnamon and sugar to half of the breadcrumbs. Now fill the dish with alternate layers of apples, cinnamon flavoured breadcrumbs and raisins. Mix the syrup with the warm water and pour over the pudding. Cover with the remaining breadcrumbs and bake at 180°C, 350°F, gas mark 4 for about an hour.

ALMOND PUDDING

This recipe comes from *The "Pudding Lady's" Recipe Book* (1917) by Florence Petty.

2 oz breadcrumbs
2 oz margarine
1½ oz sugar
2 oz sweet almonds (ground)

1 oz candied peel
(chopped)
1 teacup milk
1 egg (beaten)

Cream the margarine and sugar. Add egg and other ingredients. Bake in a greased pie-dish 30 to 40 minutes.
Serve with custard.

****

BOUDOIR PUDDING

Boudoir biscuits are the same as sponge fingers, Savoiardi biscuits, and in the USA, lady fingers.

900 ml milk
50 g ratafia biscuits
50 g boudoir biscuits
110 g butter
25 g ground almonds

2 egg yolks
1 tablespoon white wine
pinch nutmeg
sugar to taste

Place the ratafia and boudoir biscuits in a pan. Add the milk, and bring to the boil. Add the butter, and allow to melt, then set it on one side to cool. Mix the almonds with the egg yolks and add the white wine, nutmeg and sugar to taste. Mix all together and pour the mixture into a buttered dish. Bake for about 30 minutes in an oven preheated to 180°C, 350°F, gas mark 4.

FRIAR'S OMELETTE

350 g cooking apples, peeled,
cored and chopped
4 tablespoons sugar,
plus 1 teaspoon
1 tablespoon lemon juice

2 teaspoons grated lemon rind
1 egg, beaten
90 g soft breadcrumbs
15 g butter
½ teaspoon cinnamon

Put the apples in a pan and add 70 ml water, the 4 tablespoons sugar, lemon juice and grated lemon rind. Cook gently until the apple is soft. Remove from the heat and stir in the egg.

Grease an 18 cm ovenproof dish with butter and place half of the breadcrumbs in the bottom. Top with the apple mixture.

In a small pan, melt the butter and add the remaining breadcrumbs to it. Add the 1 teaspoon sugar and sprinkle over the cinnamon. Mix well then spread this mixture over the apples.

Bake at 190°C, 375°F, gas mark 5 for about 25 to 30 minutes. Serve with custard or cream.

College Puddings

Oxford and Cambridge colleges are famous for their puddings in many varieties and almost every college has a pudding named after it. Generally they are suet based with breadcrumbs, dried fruit and often with eggs and milk.

The recipe below comes from Mrs Beeton's *Book of Household Management* (1861) and seems to be a version from New College Oxford.

Ingredients. – 1 pint of bread crumbs, 6 oz. of finely-chopped suet, $1/4$ lb. of currants, a few thin slices of candied peel, 3 oz. of sugar, $1/4$ nutmeg, 3 eggs, 4 tablespoonfuls of brandy.

Mode. – Put the breadcrumbs into a basin; add the suet, currants, candied peel, sugar, and nutmeg, grated, and stir these ingredients until they are thoroughly mixed. Beat up the eggs, moisten the pudding with these, and put in the brandy; beat well for a few minutes, then form the mixture into round balls or egg-shaped pieces; fry these in hot butter or lard, letting them stew in it until thoroughly done, and turn them two or three times, till of a fine light brown; drain them on a piece of blotting paper before the fire; dish, and serve with wine sauce.

Mrs Beeton does not give a wine sauce, so here is Olive Green's 'Wine Sauce No. III' from her book *Everyday Desserts* (1911).

Beat the yolks of six eggs with three tablespoonfuls of powdered sugar [icing], the grated rind and juice of a lemon, and two wineglassfuls of wine. Cook slowly until it is a thick yellow froth, beating constantly. It must not boil and must be served immediately.

RICE AND MILK PUDDINGS

'In England we use to make with milke and rice a certaine food or pottage which doth both meanly binde the belly, and also nourish. Many other good kindes of food is made with this graine, as those that are skilfull in cookerie can tell.'

John Gerard, *Herbal*, 2nd edition, 1633

As with bread puddings, there are many variations on the rice pudding theme.

ROBERT MAY

An early recipe for rice pudding comes from a great cook of long ago, Robert May in his book *The Accomplish't Cook* (1685).

To make a Rice Pudding to bake.
Boil the race [rice] tender in milk, then season it with nutmeg, mace, rose-water, sugar, yolks of eggs, with half the whites, some grated bread, and marrow minced with ambergreese, and bake it in a buttered dish.

****

HANNAH GLASSE

Hannah in *The Art of Cookery Made Plain and Easy* (1747) has several rice puddings. This is a particularly rich one.

A Rice Pudding
Take a quarter of a Pound of Rice, put it into a Sauce-pan, with a Quart of new Milk, a Stock of Cinnamon, stir it often to keep it from sticking to the Sauce-pan. When it is boiled thick, pour it into a Pan, and stir in a quarter of a Pound of fresh butter, and Sugar to your Palate; grate in half a Nutmeg, and add three

or four Spoonfuls of Rose-water, stir all well together; when it is cold, beat up eight Eggs, with half the Whites, beat it all well together, butter a Dish and pour it in, and bake it. You may lay a Puff-paste first all over the Dish; for Change put in a few Currans and Sweetmeats, if you chuse it.

****

MEG DODS

Meg gives several rice puddings in her book, *Cook and Housewife's Manual* (1829). Here are two of them.

Delicate small rice-puddings. – Prepare four ounces of rice as above directed, and put to it three ounces of fresh butter, and a half-pint of cream. When cold, mix in sugar to taste, and six well-beat yolks of eggs, with three whites, grated lemon peel, and a little cinnamon. Butter small cups, and putting into each a few slices of candied citron, fill very nearly full, and bake them. Dish and serve them with sweet sauce in a boat.

****

GEORGE PUDDING

The combination of rice and apples was a popular one in the past. Here is a version from Meg:

A George-pudding. – Boil as for rice-pudding four ounces of rice with a roll of lemon peel. Mix this, when drained dry, with the pulp of a dozen boiled, roasted, or baked apples, well beaten. Add the beat yolks of five or six eggs, sugar to taste, and a little cinnamon, with two ounces of candied orange and citron-peel sliced. Line and butter a basin or mould with paste (not too thick,) and pour the pudding into it; then gently stir on the white of the eggs beaten to a strong froth. Bake the pudding for more than half-hour, and serve it with hot sauce made of wine, sugar, the yolk of an egg, and a bit of butter.

****

LEMON RICE

This recipe comes from May Little's *A Year's Dinners*.

3 oz rice
2 eggs
1 pint milk
1 lemon
little apricot jam
1 oz sugar

Cook the rice in the milk with the grated lemon rind. When quite tender add the well-beaten yolks of eggs, sugar and lemon juice, put it in a buttered pie dish, cook in the oven till firm, spread over a thin layer of apricot jam. Make a meringue with the whipped white of egg, pile on the top and crisp in the oven.

Pear Condé

This is a rather grand and elaborate rice pudding. It is one of the great classic French desserts. It can be made from other fruits such as apricots. The recipe is rather long and complicated but it makes an impressive dessert for a special occasion. It is served cold.

110 g short grain rice
850 ml milk
250 g sugar
25 g butter
good pinch of salt
1 teaspoon vanilla essence
6 egg yolks, lightly beaten
1 kg firm, aromatic pears
1 teaspoon vegetable oil
225 ml water
3 tablespoons brandy

Wash the rice well and then soak in cold water for about 30 minutes. Preheat the oven to 150°C, 300°F gas mark 2.

Drain the rice well and place in a large flameproof casserole. Add the milk, 50 g of the sugar, the butter, salt and vanilla essence. Place the casserole over a moderate heat and bring the mixture to a boil, stirring constantly.

Cover the casserole and transfer to the preheated oven. Bake for one hour or until the rice is tender and all the liquid has been absorbed. Remove from the oven.

Stir the egg yolks into the rice and place the casserole over a low heat. Cook gently, stirring constantly for about 3 minutes. Remove the casserole from the heat, set to one side and leave to cool.

Now prepare the pears. Peel, halve and core them. Then take about one-quarter of the pear halves and thinly slice them. Set aside.

Lightly grease a soufflé dish with the oil. When the rice mixture is cool, spoon about one-third of it into the soufflé dish. Place half the thinly sliced pears on top. Continue making layers of rice and sliced pears until used up finishing up with a layer of rice. Cover the dish with tin foil and place it in the refrigerator to chill for about 2 hours or until the rice mixture is firm.

Meanwhile, make the sauce. In a medium-sized saucepan, dissolve the remaining sugar in the water over a moderate heat, stirring constantly. Add the remaining pear halves and reduce the heat to low. Simmer until the pears are tender (about 12 to 15 minutes). Remove the pan from the heat.

Remove half of the pears from the pan with a slotted spoon and set them to one side. Puree the remaining pears halves with the syrup. Return the puree to the pan and place the pan over a high heat bringing to the boil. Boil for about 3 minutes.

Remove the pan from the heat and stir in the brandy. Pour the sauce into a bowl and leave to cool. When cool enough put in the refrigerator to chill for about 30 minutes.

When ready to serve, remove the soufflé dish containing the rice from the refrigerator. Remove the foil and place a serving dish, inverted, over the soufflé dish and reverse the two. The pudding should come out easily.

Arrange the reserved pear halves on the top and around the sides. Serve the sauce separately.

RICE PUDDING EASTERN-STYLE

In Afghanistan a rice pudding called *sheer birinj* is sometimes served as a dessert for special occasions.

110 g short grain rice
570 ml water
500 ml milk
110 g sugar
2 teaspoons rosewater
1/4 teaspoon ground green cardamom seeds
25 g ground pistachio and/or almonds

Wash the rice and put in a pan, add the water, bring to the bowl, then turn down the heat to medium and boil gently until the rice is cooked and soft and all the water has evaporated. Stir from time to time to prevent the rice from sticking.

Add the milk and bring back to the boil, then turn down the heat again and boil gently until the mixture thickens a little bit, then add the sugar. Continue to boil gently, stirring often to prevent sticking, until the sugar has dissolved and the mixture has thickened, although still runny.

Add the ground cardamom and the rosewater and cook for another 1 or 2 minutes.

Serve the rice on a large flat plate, decorated with the pistachios and almonds.

Serve warm or cold.

SEMOLINA PUDDING

568 ml milk
4 level tablespoons semolina
75 g sugar
2 teaspoons cinnamon
grated rind of ½ lemon
50 g raisins
2 eggs separated
slivered almonds and pistachios

Heat the milk, sprinkle on the semolina, stir and bring to the boil. Cook for two or three minutes, stirring constantly to avoid sticking and burning. Remove from the heat and stir in half the sugar, the cinnamon, lemon rind, raisins and egg yolks and pour into an ovenproof dish. Whisk the egg whites stiffly, fold in the remaining sugar and pile on top of the pudding. Stud with the almonds and pistachios. Bake in the oven at 200°C, 400°F, gas mark 6 for about five or ten minutes, until the meringue is lightly browned.

SWEET MACARONI PUDDING

H ere is another pudding from *Mrs Beeton's Book of Household Management* (1861).

INGREDIENTS.- 2½ oz. of macaroni, 2 pints of milk, the rind of ½ lemon, 3 eggs, sugar and grated nutmeg to taste, 2 tablespoons of brandy.

MODE.- Put the macaroni, with a pint of the milk, into a saucepan with the lemon-peel, and let it simmer gently until the macaroni is tender; then put it into a pie-dish, without the peel; mix the other pint of milk with the eggs; stir these well together, adding the sugar and brandy, and pour the mixture over the macaroni. Grate a little nutmeg over the top, and bake in a moderate oven for ½ hour. To make this pudding look nice, a paste should be laid round the edges of the dish, and, for variety, a layer of preserve or marmalade may be placed on the macaroni: in this case omit the brandy.

VERMICELLI MILK PUDDING

This is called *sheer semiyan* in Afghanistan. In the East puddings tend to be sweet so the amount of sugar can be reduced if wished.

75 g vermicelli
1 tablespoon ghee or vegetable oil
500 ml whole milk
2 level tablespoons cornflour
200 g sugar
1 tablespoon rosewater
1/2 teaspoon cardamom
1 tablespoon ground pistachio

Break up the vermicelli into 5 cm lengths. Fry gently in the ghee or oil until well coated and golden brown. Bring a pot of water to the boil and add the vermicelli. Boil gently for a couple of minutes until just soft. Drain in a colander and set to one side.

Mix the cornflour to a paste with a little of the milk. Heat the remaining milk adding the cornflour paste slowly and stir constantly until the milk thickens. Add the sugar, rosewater and cardamom, stir well and simmer for about 2 minutes. Now add the vermicelli to the milk, mix well and pour onto a shallow serving dish. Sprinkle with the pistachio and allow to cool.

The following two recipes from Olive Green's *Everyday Desserts* bear no resemblance to any memories I have of eating these puddings at school dinners.

STRAWBERRY TAPIOCA PUDDING

Soak over-night a cupful of tapioca in cold water to cover. Simmer until clear in a double boiler with sufficient salted water. Butter a deep baking-dish and fill with alternate layers of tapioca and strawberries, sprinkling each layer of the fruit with sugar. Have tapioca on top. Sprinkle with sugar, dot with butter, and bake for forty minutes in a moderate oven. Serve cold with cream or boiled custard. Peaches, apples, pineapple, cherries, or other fruits may be used in the same way. Strawberries combined with bananas make a delicious pudding.

****

SAGO PUDDING

Heat a quart of milk in a double boiler and cook in it until soft three-fourths cupful of sago. Add two tablespoonfuls of butter, one cupful of sugar, and flavouring to taste. Cool, add the well-beaten yolks of four eggs, turn into a buttered baking dish, and bake for thirty of forty minutes. Spread jam over the pudding, cover with a meringue made of the stiffly beaten whites, return to the oven until puffed and brown, and serve cold.

RASPBERRY BATTER PUDDING

This is similar to the French dish, clafoutis, which is often made with cherries. This recipe uses raspberries but other fruits could be used such as plums, apricots, etc.

3 eggs
50 g sugar
50 g plain flour
300 ml whole milk
225 g raspberries
icing sugar

Grease an ovenproof dish with butter.

Whisk the eggs and sugar until pale and frothy. Sift in the flour and stir well. Add the milk and mix well.

Arrange the fruit in the bottom of the greased dish. Pour over the batter and bake at 200°C, 400°F, gas mark 6 for about 30 minutes until cooked and golden brown.

Serve hot, dredged with icing sugar.

MALVERN PUDDING

It was thought by many that this pudding had been 'lost'. In fact the original recipe dating from the 1880s is safely preserved at the Malvern Museum and here it is.

Base
1 lb cooking apples
1 oz butter
1 oz granulated sugar
Grated rind of 1 small lemon

Sauce
1 standard egg
1 oz butter
1 oz cornflour
3/4 pint milk
1 oz granulated sugar

Topping
2 oz demerara sugar
1/2 level teaspoon cinnamon
1/2 oz butter

Method

1. Peel, core and slice apples. Melt butter in a medium sized saucepan. Add apples and 1 oz sugar. Cover and cook over a low heat, stirring occasionally until soft and thick. Add lemon rind and put mixture into a 1 1/2 pint ovenproof dish.

2. Beat egg. Melt 1 oz butter in saucepan. Stir in flour and cook gently for about 2 minutes without browning. Add milk, bring to the boil, stirring. Simmer for 2 minutes. Remove from heat and stir in 1 oz sugar. Beat in egg a little at a time. Return to heat and cook for 1 minute, stirring. Pour sauce over apple mixture.

3. Mix demerara sugar and cinnamon together. Sprinkle on top of sauce and dot with 1/2 oz butter. Place dish under a moderate grill and heat until sugar has caramelized. Serve hot or cold.

LIST OF RECIPES

SOME BOOKS CONSULTED

Adam's Luxury, and Eve's Cookery, facsimile edn (1744), Prospect Books Ltd, London, 1983

The Dairy Book of British Food, Ebury Press, London, 1988

[Glasse, Hannah], *The Art of Cookery Made Plain and Easy*, by 'A Lady', facsimile reprint (1747), Prospect Books, Totnes, 1995

Acton, Eliza, *Modern Cookery for Private Families*, Longman, Green, Longman and Roberts, 1845

Baily, Adrian (ed), *The Cooking of the British Isles*, Time-Life Int., Netherlands, 1971

Beeton, Mrs Isabella, *The Book of Household Management*, facsimile edn (1861), Jonathan Cape, London, 1968

Dallas, E. S., *Kettner's Book of the Table* (1877), Centaur Press, London, 1968

Davidson, Alan, *The Oxford Companion to Food*, Oxford University Press, Oxford, 1999

Dods, Mistress Margaret, *The Cook and Housewife's Manual* (1829) 4th edn, facsimile reprint, Rosters Ltd, London, 1988

F.K., *The Everyday Pudding Book*, Stanley Paul, London, n.d.

Good Housekeeping Institute, *Good Housekeeping Cookery Book*, Ebury Press, London, 1978

Green, Olive, *Everyday Desserts*, G P Putnam's Sons, New York, 1911

Grossman, Anne Chotzinoff and Thomas, Lisa Grossman, *Lobscouse and Spotted Dog*, W. W. Norton, New York, 2000

Kenney-Herbert, Col, *Culinary Jottings for Madras by "Wyvern" [fifth edition]*, (Madras,1885), facsimile reprint, Prospect Books, Totnes, 1994

Lessels, Julie (ed), *The Etiquette of English Puddings*, Copper Beech Publishing, East Grinstead, 1996

Little, May, *A Year's Dinners*, T. Werner Laurie, London, n.d.

Mason, Laura, *Farmhouse Cookery*, The National Trust, London, 2005

May, Robert, *The Accomplish't Cook* (1685) facsimile reprint, Prospect Books, Totnes, 1994

Petty, Florence, *The "Pudding Lady's" Recipe Book*, G. Bell & Sons, London, 1917

Raffald, Elizabeth, *The Experienced English Housekeeper* (1769) reprint, Southover Press, Lewes, 1997

The WI and Smith, Michael, *A Cook's Tour of Britain*, Willow Books, London, 1984

Tickletooth, Tabitha, *The Dinner Question*, facsimile reprint (1860), Prospect Books, Totnes, 1999

White, Florence, *Good Things in England*, Jonathon Cape, London, 1932

Wilson, C. Anne (ed), *Traditional Foods East and West of the Pennines*, Edinburgh University Press, Edinburgh, 1991